CANADA: THE LAND
EXPLORING CANADA
Lynda Sorensen

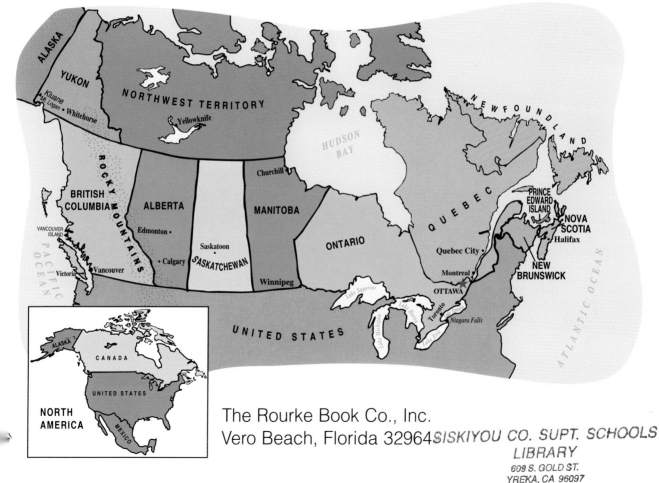

The Rourke Book Co., Inc.
Vero Beach, Florida 32964

Edited by Sandra A. Robinson and
Pamela J.P. Schroeder

PHOTO CREDITS
All photos © Lynn M. Stone except page 21 © Jerry Hennen

Library of Congress Cataloging-in-Publication Data

Sorensen, Lynda, 1953-
  Canada: the land / by Lynda Sorensen.
    p. cm. — (Exploring Canada)
  Includes index.
  ISBN 1-55916-106-X
  1. Canada—Geography—Juvenile literature. [1. Canada—
Geography.] I. Title. II. Series.
F1011.3.S67   1995
917.1—dc20   94-46853
                                              CIP
                                              AC

Printed in the USA

TABLE OF CONTENTS

CANADA: THE LAND

Canada is a country with beautiful scenery and many natural resources. Towering mountains and waterfalls, **glaciers,** wild rivers, great forests and a huge carpet of **tundra** lie within Canada's borders.

Canada is the largest country in North America, and second only to Russia in the world. Canada stretches 3,223 miles (5,187 kilometers) from the Pacific Ocean to the Atlantic Ocean. It reaches 2,875 miles (4,627 kilometers) from Lake Erie north into the Arctic Ocean.

SEASHORES

Imagine hiking around the Earth's middle six times. That's how long Canada's seashore is— 151,488 miles (243,797 kilometers)!

Most of Canada's coast is the distance around hundreds of sea islands. Several huge Arctic islands such as Victoria, Baffin and Ellesmere are among them.

Canada's seashore is wide and sandy in places. In other places it's lined with rocks or steep cliffs.

Canada's seashore includes the rocky, icy coast along Hudson Bay in northern Manitoba

MOUNTAINS

Much of western Canada is a land in the clouds, a land of high mountain peaks and rugged foothills.

The Rocky Mountains reach from Canada's southern border with the United States north into the Yukon. West of the Rockies, the Coast Mountains hug the Pacific Ocean. Mount Logan in the Coast Mountains is Canada's tallest peak—at 19,524 feet (5,951 meters) above sea level.

Mountains also tower above some of the Arctic islands. Several smaller peaks rise in eastern Canada.

Aspen trees in Canada's mountain parks turn gold in the fall

LAKES AND RIVERS

Hundreds of rivers rush through Canada, and thousands of lakes sparkle like blue gems.

The St. Lawrence River in eastern Canada is a busy waterway between the Atlantic Ocean and the Great Lakes.

Canada shares four Great Lakes—Superior, Huron, Erie and Ontario—with the United States. Two other huge lakes, Great Bear and Great Slave, lie in the Northwest Territories.

On maps, Hudson Bay looks like a giant lake. It's really a giant thumb of the ocean that dips hundreds of miles into Canada.

Red salmon swim up a clear, wild river in British Columbia

Canada's forest ends where its tundra begins

Rocks guard the New Brunswick seashore in eastern Canada

FORESTS

Forests cover nearly half of Canada. Most of the trees are evergreens—firs, spruces, pines and cedars.

Ontario has forests of evergreens mixed with broad-leaved trees. Broad-leaved trees—like aspens, maples and birches—lose their leaves each autumn.

The Canadian forest has fewer trees in the cold North, where pockets of swamp and open, grassy ground appear.

Thick evergreen forests cover much of central and southern Canada

TUNDRA

In Canada's Far North, the forest stops, and the tundra begins. The tundra is a treeless mat of low-lying plants. It sweeps across almost all of northern Canada.

Permafrost is frozen ground that lies just a few inches beneath the windy tundra. Permafrost is *always* frozen, so tree roots cannot grow in it.

Each summer the tundra is a colorful meadow of wildflowers, grasses and strange little plants called **lichens.**

Snow geese raise their young on the tundra in the Northwest Territories

PRAIRIES

For thousands of years, wild grasses covered much of the southern **prairie provinces.** Fires and the dense roots of the wild plants kept trees from growing there.

Parts of southern Alberta, Saskatchewan and Manitoba are still prairies, or grasslands.

Much of the Canadian prairie has been plowed for farm land. However, thousands of little ponds, called **potholes,** remain. They were made by glaciers that moved across the land long ago.

Parts of the prairie provinces are still covered in wildflowers and wild grasses

GLACIERS

Glaciers are huge, slow-moving masses of ice. They no longer grind across the Canadian prairies. Today, many glaciers cling to the cold, snowy Canadian peaks.

Athabasca Glacier lies within a few steps of the Icefields Parkway in Jasper National Park, Alberta. Each summer, thousands of visitors walk to the edge of mighty Athabasca. A snow coach takes people for a ride on the glacier's blue ice.

Salmon Glacier is one of several hundred glaciers in Canada

CLIMATE

Climate is the kind of weather a place has year after year. Canada is so large that it has several different climates. Almost all of Canada, though, has cold, snowy winters and mild summers with long periods of sunshine.

Arctic Canada—the most northern part—is very dry, windy and icy cold during the winter. Summers there are mild, but short.

Most of Canada's southern coastal areas have heavy rainfall and fog.

Glossary

glacier (GLAY shur) — a massive river of ice

lichen (LIE kin) — rootless, plantlike growths made up of alga and fungus

permafrost (PER muh frawst) — ground frozen year-round

pothole (PAHT hole) — a small, round pond of the North American prairies

prairie (PRAIR ree) — natural grassland, especially in western and midwestern North America

province (PRAH vints) — any one of the 10 statelike regions, which together with two territories, make up Canada

tundra (TUN druh) — the treeless carpet of low-lying plants in the Far North and on mountains above the tree line

INDEX

Native Americans

The Nez Perce

Richard M. Gaines

ABDO Publishing Company

visit us at
www.abdopub.com

Published by ABDO Publishing Company, 4940 Viking Drive, Suite 622, Edina, Minnesota 55435. Copyright © 2000 Abdo Consulting Group, Inc., Pentagon Tower, P.O. Box 36036, Minneapolis, Minnesota 55435 USA. International copyrights reserved in all countries. No part of this book may be reproduced in any form without written permission from the publisher.

Printed in the United States.

Illustrator: David Fadden (pgs. 9, 11, 13, 17, 19, 20, 23)
Cover Photo: Corbis
Interior Photos: Corbis (pgs. 4, 7, 10, 14, 15, 24, 27, 28, 29, 30)
Editors: Bob Italia, Tamara L. Britton, Kate A. Furlong
Art Direction & Maps: Pat Laurel
Border Design: Carey Molter/MacLean & Tuminelly (Mpls.)

Library of Congress Cataloging-in-Publication Data

Gaines, Richard M., 1942-
   The Nez Perce / Richard M. Gaines.
     p. cm. -- (Native Americans)
   Includes bibliographical references and index.
   Summary: Presents a brief introduction to the Nez Perce Indians including information on their society, homes, food, clothing, crafts, and life today.
   ISBN 1-57765-375-0
   1. Nez Perce Indians--Juvenile literature. [1. Nez Perce Indians. 2. Indians of North America--Northwest, Pacific.] I. Title.

E99.N5 G35 2000
979.5'0049741--dc21
                              99-059864

Contributing Editor: Barbara Gray, JD

Barbara Gray, JD (Kanatiyosh) is a member of the Mohawk Nation (Akwesasne), which is in New York State and Canada. Barbara earned her Juris Doctorate from Arizona State University College of Law in May of 1999. She is presently pursuing a Doctorate in Justice Studies that focuses on American Indian culture and issues at Arizona State University. When she finishes school, she will return home to the Mohawk Nation.

Illustrator: David Kanietakeron Fadden

David Kanietakeron Fadden is a member of the Akwesasne Mohawk Wolf Clan. His work has appeared in publications such as *Akwesasne Notes, Indian Time*, and the *Northeast Indian Quarterly*. Examples of his work have also appeared in various publications of the Six Nations Indian Museum in Onchiota, NY. His work has also appeared in "How The West Was Lost: Always The Enemy," produced by Gannett Production which appeared on the Discovery Channel. David's work has been exhibited in Albany, NY; the Lake Placid Center for the Arts; Centre Strathearn in Montreal, Quebec; North Country Community College in Saranac Lake, NY; Paul Smith's College in Paul Smiths, NY; and at the Unison Arts & Learning Center in New Paltz, NY.

Contents

Where They Lived

The Nez Perce (NESS PURSE) lived on the Columbia Plateau where present-day Oregon, Washington, and Idaho come together. This region is also known as the Pacific Northwest. The land has mountains, deep canyons, forests, and swift streams and rivers.

The Pacific Northwest is cold in the winter. The great snowdrifts made travel difficult and dangerous. During the winter, the Nez Perce moved down from the mountains into the warmer canyons.

The Nez Perce homelands had around 17 million acres (68,800 sq. k). It stretched west toward the Cascade Mountains and east toward the Rocky Mountains. The Nez Perce believe that they have lived in this region since the beginning of time. They call themselves the "Nimi'ipu" (NEE-ME-POO). It means "the people." The Nimi'ipu speak a **Sahaptin** language.

The land of the Nez Perce

In the 1600s, the Shoshoni told French-Canadian traders about a pierced-nosed people who wore shell jewelry. The traders decided to look for these people.

The French-Canadians soon found the Nimi'ipu. They called them Nez Perce. This means "drilled nose" or "pierced-nose." It is not known if the Nimi'ipu actually had pierced noses. But, from that day forward, they were known as the Nez Perce.

The Nez Perce lived in the Columbia Plateau region of the Pacific Northwest.

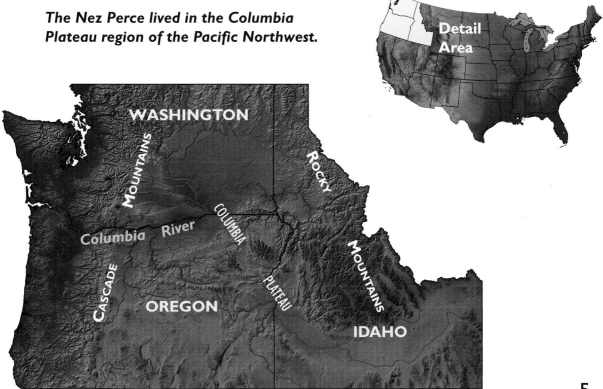

Society

The Nez Perce were the largest Native American tribe in the Pacific Northwest. They numbered about 6,000 in 1800. They were divided among about 80 separate **bands** of related families. The bands settled next to the rivers and formed villages. The villages were often named after the river the band settled next to.

Each band had a "headman," or chief. This headman was an **elder**. Headmen were usually decided by **heredity**. In a large village, there was a headman, a peace leader, and a war leader. Sometimes, the headman was a **medicine man**. He healed the sick and performed **ceremonies**.

The Nez Perce believed all their people should help make important decisions. They selected three or four members to sit on the village council along with the leaders. The council worked to do what was best for the people.

Owning property was uncommon. Instead, many families shared one home. Anyone could use it as shelter. When a man died, band members received his possessions.

The Nez Perce thought lying was a sin and an insult. Their language had no curse words. The worst thing one could say about a person was that he or she was "kap-seese," or no-good.

A Nez Perce headman

Homes

The Nez Perce lived in tipis, longhouses, and pit houses.

In the late 1600s, the Shoshoni introduced the Nez Perce to the horse. Horses helped the Nez Perce travel greater distances. They could trade with the Native Americans of the **Great Plains**. This activity introduced the Nez Perce to the tipi.

Tipis were made of 12 wooden poles. These poles formed an upside-down, cone-shaped frame. The frame was covered with buffalo hides that were sewn together. The tipi was ideal for traveling. It was easy to set up and break down. And, horses could pull tipis on **travois**.

The Nez Perce built longhouses by digging a hole the length and width of the house. Then, they built an A-shaped frame over the hole. It supported the roof and walls.

The roof and walls were made from woven cattail and reed mats. These materials were tied to the frame. Longhouses could be more than 100 feet (30 m) long. They housed many families. Longhouses were also used for **ceremonies**.

Longhouses were good winter homes. Each had several fire pits and smoke holes. The fires kept the entire home warm. The sides had many doors that allowed the families to come and go. Beds were placed along the walls. Mattresses were made with layers of dry grass and cottonwood bark.

The Nez Perce built pit houses by digging a round, five-foot (1.5-m) hole. Then, a frame was built over the hole to support the roof and walls. This frame was covered with woven reed mats. Ladders helped people get in and out of the house. Pit houses were used along with longhouses. Single men and women also lived in them.

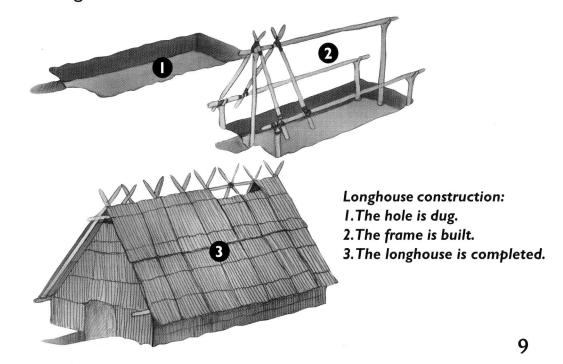

Longhouse construction:
1. The hole is dug.
2. The frame is built.
3. The longhouse is completed.

Food

One-year-old Snake River sockeye salmon

Salmon are born in the fresh waters of the Snake, Salmon, and Clearwater Rivers of the Pacific Northwest. The baby salmon then float downstream into the Pacific Ocean. A few years later, the adult salmon return to **spawn** in the same rivers where they were born.

The Nez Perce waited for the first returning salmon in early spring. When the fish were sighted, a First Feast **Ceremony** was performed. The ceremony thanked the Great Spirit and the fish for giving its life. During the ceremony, no fishing was allowed. The salmon were allowed to return to their river home to spawn.

After the First Feast Ceremony, the Nez Perce began to catch the salmon. They used spears, lines and hooks, fiber-woven traps, and nets. Some fishermen stood on wooden platforms. Other fishermen waded into the river. Trout and sturgeon were also caught. Fishing season ran from spring until fall.

Some fish were eaten fresh. Others were dried for winter use. The women placed the cleaned fish on a drying rack built above a fire. The smoke preserved the fish. They were eaten all winter long.

In the summer, the women gathered strawberries, elderberries, blackberries, huckleberries, and gooseberries. Flowers were eaten fresh and dried for the winter. The Nez Perce mixed fruits, meat, and fat. This dried mixture was eaten in the winter and when traveling.

The women also went to the prairies in search of food. They used sticks to dig up bitterroot, wild carrot, wild potato, and camas root. The camas bulb was eaten raw, which was sweet and crunchy. Or, it could be dried for later use. Roasted camas was made into mush and loaves. A First Feast **Ceremony** in the spring thanked the plants for providing the Nez Perce with food.

The Nez Perce hunted deer, elk, bear, mountain goat, buffalo, and pronghorn antelope with bows and arrows. They trapped rabbits, squirrels, and birds.

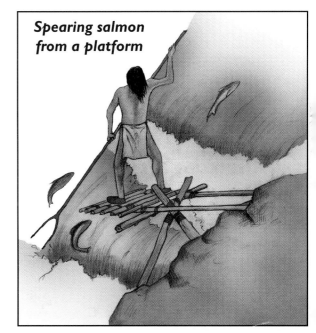

Spearing salmon from a platform

Clothing

Men wore fringed shirts, breechcloths, leggings, gloves, and moccasins. The clothes were made of **tanned** deer or elk skins.

Shirt sleeves had long fringes along their undersides. The seams and **hem** had shorter fringes. Shirts also had a V-shape below the head opening. It had short fringes and a **rosette** design. Shirts were also decorated with porcupine quills. Sometimes, the fringes were quilled, too.

Women wore long buckskin dresses, knee-length moccasins, leggings, and woven hats. The dresses hung from the shoulders to the ankles. They were gathered at the waist with a belt. Long fringes hung from the underside of the sleeves and from the hem. The dresses were decorated with porcupine quills, elk teeth, and tusk shells. This long, tube-like shell was also worn as jewelry.

Knee-length moccasins were decorated with porcupine quills. Basketry hats were cone-shaped. They were woven with plant fibers. After they began trading with Europeans, the Nez Perce also used glass beads to decorate their clothing.

Each Nez Perce man became known by the way he braided his hair. Each cut his hair above the eyes so it stood high and fell a little to the side. Men and women often painted their faces bright red and yellow for **ceremonies**.

A Nez Perce family in traditional dress. The baby is on a cradleboard.

Crafts

The Nez Perce are famous for their weaving, quilling, and beadwork.

Women wove baskets used for gathering berries and roots. These baskets were also used to store food and hold water. Hot rocks were placed inside the baskets to heat the water.

Nez Perce women wove a rounded, cone-shaped hat. They used hemp, grass, and cedar root **fibers** to make them. Dark-colored plant fibers were used for designs. Sometimes, leather or quill tassels were attached.

The quill worker used her mouth and teeth to soften and flatten each quill. Before the quill dried and became hard, it was carefully sewn into place.

A woman's cone-shaped hat

The quill worker used **geometric** shapes to decorate the clothing. The women colored their quills with dyes from the juice of berries, trees, and minerals. The women put quill work on leggings, **cradleboard** coverings, moccasins, and dresses.

Men wove fishing nets from plant fibers. They made bows from ash, willow wood, or the horn of a bighorn sheep.

Quilled moccasins

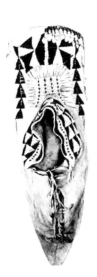

A cradleboard with quillwork design

A man's quilled shirt

Family

Men married at about 14 years old. Women married even younger. Their families arranged the marriages.

The bride was led to the groom's family's house. Each family had a celebration for the newly married couple. Sometimes, the groom gave the bride's father wild game and fish. This showed he was a good provider. Sometimes, the bride gave the groom's family beautiful clothing. This showed she was good at making clothes.

A number of families often lived in one house. If a child was **orphaned**, another family could care for it.

The women cared for the home. They also gathered food, cooked, made baskets, and decorated the family clothing.

The men hunted, fished, cared for the horses, and cut firewood. They also set up the pit houses and longhouses.

Families often traveled together to hunt buffalo. They went to the prairies east of Nez Perce homelands. Sometimes, hunting trips lasted for a year or more.

A Nez Perce woman weaves a basket.

Children

Newborn children spent most of their time on a wooden **cradleboard**. Cradleboards hug babies tight. This makes them feel safe and happy.

The Nez Perce cradleboard has a rounded top and a pointy bottom. The baby is bundled in soft furs. A covering is attached to the board. It is pulled tightly around the baby and laced up.

Mothers and grandmothers taught the older children to be quiet and respectful. Grandmothers spent much time with children. They told them stories. These stories taught the children Nez Perce history and lessons about life.

The children helped the women pick berries and gather roots. The Nez Perce believed that children learned best by helping their parents. Girls learned how to quill, make clothing, care for the babies, and prepare food. The men taught boys how to hunt and fish. They also learned to take care of and ride their horses.

The Nez Perce are famous for their Appaloosas. These horses were valuable trade items. The native people and Europeans admired the horses' beauty. Appaloosas are still **bred** today.

Nez Perce boys learning to ride Appaloosas

Myths

A young tribal member on a vision quest encounters her secret spirit.

Tribal members could earn a third and secret name on a **vision quest**. Relatives would leave young members on a mountain for three days and nights. A spirit, dream, or animal would teach the children a song. It would also give them their secret spirit name. No one ever told their secret name to anyone else. But, at special Guardian Spirit Dances, the Nez Perce would sing the songs the spirits had taught them.

Sometimes **myths** teach lessons. Sometimes they entertain. Sometimes myths do both. The following is the Nez Perce creation story. It teaches that man and nature are related.

A long time ago, before humans were created, a giant monster crawled upon the earth. It swallowed animals, plants, and even rocks. Coyote saw what was going on. He knew he needed to help the animals that had been swallowed.

Coyote said a prayer to the Great Spirit. He asked for courage and wisdom. The Great Spirit reminded Coyote of his guardian spirit, the grape vine. Then, Coyote knew what to do.

Coyote tied one end of the grape vine around his middle. Then, he tied the other end to a tree. Coyote hid a sharpened bone knife in his mouth.

Coyote stood bravely in front of the monster. It swallowed him whole. The monster's big teeth broke the vine. Coyote began to fall.

Just as he reached the monster's heart, Coyote acted quickly. He removed the knife from his mouth and cut out the monster's heart. The monster fell dead with its mouth wide open. Coyote and all the other animals ran out.

The Great Spirit told Coyote to make good use of the monster. The coyote began to cut up the body. Each piece created a new tribe of people. Then, Coyote squeezed the blood from the heart. From this blood, the Great Spirit created the Nez Perce.

War

The Nez Perce were the most peaceful Native American tribe in the Pacific Northwest. They were honest and gentle people. They only went to war to protect their land and people.

The Nez Perce went to war against other Native Americans after the Europeans arrived in America. By then, the Nez Perce depended on the fur trade for survival. They needed animal **pelts** to trade for things like blankets, tools, kettles, and guns. The Bannock and Shoshoni also wanted the animals on Nez Perce land. The Nez Perce fought to keep these peoples away.

The Nez Perce also fought wars against the United States Army. In 1855, the U.S. government wanted to open Nez Perce land to white settlers. The Nez Perce agreed to a **treaty**. It allowed them to keep 10,000 square miles (25,900 sq. k) of their homeland.

In 1860, gold was discovered on Nez Perce land. The U.S. government wanted the Nez Perce to give most of their land to the settlers and move to a **reservation**. Some Nez Perce **bands** signed the treaty. But, the Wallowa band refused.

In May 1877, the Nez Perce War began. Five Nez Perce bands fought the U.S. Army. For three months, the Nez Perce retreated from Idaho through Montana. They defeated the army in seven battles. But finally, many of the Nez Perce surrendered in the Bear Paw Mountains of Montana.

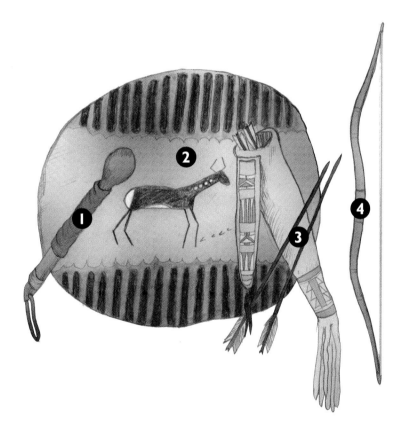

Nez Perce weapons: 1. War club 2. Shield 3. Arrows and quiver 4. Bow

Contact with Europeans

Meriwether Lewis

William Clark

The Nez Perce first contacted Europeans on September 20, 1805. That's when the Lewis and Clark **Expedition** arrived in their lands.

In 1804, the U.S. government hired Meriwether Lewis and William Clark to map much of the land acquired in the **Louisiana Purchase**. Part of this land included the Nez Perce homelands of the Pacific Northwest.

The Nez Perce welcomed Lewis and Clark into their homes. They gave them food, fresh horses, and supplies.

Lewis and Clark told the Nez Perce of their goal to reach the Pacific Ocean. The Nez Perce knew how to get to the ocean. They traded with the native peoples living along its shore.

The Nez Perce helped Lewis and Clark draw a map that would get them to the Columbia River. Then, the river would take them to the Pacific Ocean. The expedition reached the ocean in November 1805.

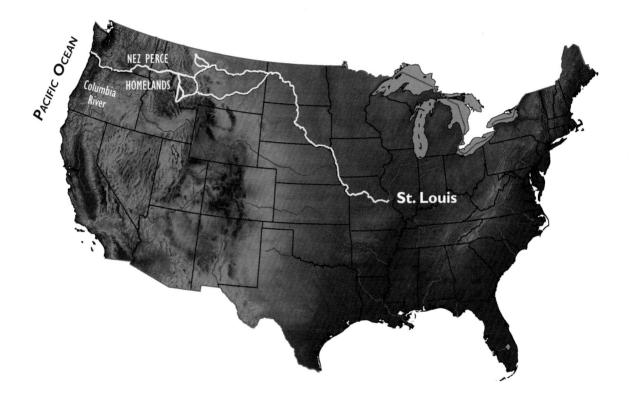

The trail of the Lewis and Clark Expedition. It started in St. Louis, Missouri, on May 14, 1804, and ended there on September 23, 1806.

Young Chief Joseph

Young Chief Joseph (Heinmot Tooyalakekt) was born in 1832. He was the son of the great chief whose Nez Perce name was Tu-ya-kas-kas. Today, the great chief is known as Old Chief Joseph.

After Old Chief Joseph died in 1871, Young Chief Joseph became leader of the Willamotkin band of the Nez Perce. Young Chief Joseph was not a war leader. He tried to keep peace and avoid war.

In 1877, the U.S. government ordered Young Chief Joseph and his people to move to the Lapwai **Reservation** in Idaho territory. They were given 30 days to leave Wallowa Valley. Young Chief Joseph refused the order.

Fights over land finally led to war in 1877. The Nez Perce won many battles against the U.S. Army. But, Young Chief Joseph knew his people could not win the war.

Young Chief Joseph decided to retreat to Canada. He led his people across the Rocky Mountains and into Montana.

By now, many Nez Perce were tired and ill. So, they made camp in the Bear Paw Mountains, only 40 miles (64 km) from Canada. The

U.S. Army found the camp and surrounded them. The Nez Perce held off the soldiers for several days. But, on October 5, 1877, Young Chief Joseph made this famous surrender speech:

"It is cold, and we have no blankets. The little children are freezing to death. My people, some of them, have run away to the hills, and have no blankets, no food. No one knows where they are—perhaps freezing to death. I want to have time to look for my children, and see how many of them I can find. Maybe I shall find them among the dead. Hear me, my chiefs! I am tired. My heart is sick and sad. From where the sun now stands, I will fight no more forever."

Young Chief Joseph

Young Chief Joseph and the Nez Perce fought no more. Most surrendered to the army when promised they could return to their homeland. Instead, the captured Nez Perce were sent to a **reservation** in Oklahoma, where many died.

In 1885, Young Chief Joseph was sent to the Colville Reservation in Nespelem, Washington. He died there on September 21, 1904.

The Nez Perce Today

As of June 2000, there were 3,300 members of the Nez Perce Tribe. They live on the Nez Perce **Reservation** in Kamiah, Idaho. The tribal headquarters is in Lapwai, Idaho. There are also Nez Perce on the Colville Reservation in Nespelem, Washington.

Part of the **traditional** Nez Perce homelands in Oregon have been turned into a national park called the Eagle Cap Wilderness. No roads have been built there. No cars or trucks are allowed. The park looks like it did when the Nez Perce called it home. The Nez Perce own nearly 50,000 acres (202 sq. k). The Nez Perce Tribal Executive **Committee** oversees this land.

The Eagle Cap Wilderness

A young Nez Perce girl wearing a beaded poncho with seashells

The Nez Perce use a **committee** style of government. Tribal members elect people every three years. There are nine members of the Nez Perce Tribal Executive Committee.

Many Nez Perce have graduated from college. They are keeping their culture alive. The Chief Joseph Foundation has a Nez Perce Mounted Scholars Program. The program combines math, reading, and writing classes with the study of Nez Perce **culture**.

Children between the ages of eight and fourteen can join the program. The children learn about Nez Perce history. And, they learn how to ride and take care of Appaloosa horses.

Carla High Eagle of the Nez Perce Reservation leads her children home on her Appaloosa

The Nez Perce also celebrate their **culture** during the Chief Lookingglass **Pow-wow**. It is held every August at the Nez Perce **Reservation**.

The pow-wow is named for Nez Perce chief Lookingglass. In 1877, he led 300 Nez Perce from certain capture in Montana by U.S. troops to safety in Canada.

Besides the fancy-dress dance contest, there is a parade, a "Friendship Feast," and other activities. Visitors can buy Nez Perce arts and crafts.

Chief Lookingglass in 1877

Fancy-dress dance contest at the Chief Lookingglass Pow-wow

Glossary

band - a number of persons acting together; a subgroup of a tribe.

breed - to produce young; a group of plants or animals looking much alike and having the same type of ancestors.

ceremony - a special act to be done on special occasions.

committee - a group of persons appointed or elected to do some special thing.

cradleboard - a decorated flat board with a wooden band at the top that protects the baby's head.

culture - the customs, arts, and tools of a nation or people at a certain time.

elder - a person having authority because of age or experience.

expedition - a journey for a special purpose, such as exploration or scientific study.

fiber - a thread-like part.

geometric - made up of straight lines, circles, and other simple shapes.

Great Plains - pasture land east of the Rocky Mountains in the United States and Canada.

hem - the border or edge on a piece of clothing.

heredity - passed down to the next generation in the family.

Louisiana Purchase - the land the United States purchased from France in 1803, extending from the Mississippi River to the Rocky Mountains and from Canada to the Gulf of Mexico.

medicine man - a spiritual leader of a tribe or nation.

myth - a legend or story that tries to explain nature.

orphan - a child whose parents are dead.

pelt - an animal skin with the fur still on it.

pow-wow - a ceremony of Native Americans, usually involving feasts, dancing, and performances.

reservation - tract of land set apart by a government for Native Americans.

rosette - an ornament shaped like a rose.

Sahaptin - a family of languages spoken by the closely related tribes that lived in the area where Washington, Oregon, and Idaho meet.

spawn - to produce eggs.

tan - to make a hide into leather by soaking in a special liquid.

tradition - the handing down of beliefs, customs, and stories from parents to children.

travois - a simple vehicle used by Native Americans to move goods and people. A travois was made with two long tipi poles tied together to form a big triangle. Toward the bottom of the triangle, shorter poles were tied onto the tipi poles. The shorter poles formed a platform that carried food, children, and the elderly.

treaty - a formal agreement between nations.

vision quest - a way for Native Americans—especially young people—to communicate with nature and the spirit world. People on vision quests seek advice, answers to questions, and an understanding of why they have come to this earth.

Web sites

The official site of the Nez Perce Tribal Headquarters is **http://www.nezperce.org**

The University of Idaho Web site also has an informative section about the Nez Perce. Its "Nee-Mee-Poo (The People)" Web page can be found at **http://www.uidaho.edu/nezperce/neemepoo.htm**

These sites are subject to change. Go to your favorite search engine and type in "Nez Perce" for more sites.

Index